Original title:
Tides of the Endless Sea

Copyright © 2025 Creative Arts Management OÜ
All rights reserved.

Author: Alexander Thornton
ISBN HARDBACK: 978-1-80587-465-2
ISBN PAPERBACK: 978-1-80587-935-0

Dreaming in the Liquid Embrace

In a bubble bath, I float,
With rubber ducks, I share a boat.
Shampoo mermaids brushing hair,
While seahorse taxis spin in air.

Fish in tuxedos swim around,
Ballet dancing without a sound.
Jellyfish twirl, a graceful guise,
While crabs gossip with twinkling eyes.

The Ever-changing Portrait of the Sea.

The ocean's mood swings left and right,
Sometimes calm, sometimes a fright.
Starfish posing like actors grand,
While seaweed waves a leafy hand.

Seashells play a game of hide,
With clams peeking, but filled with pride.
Octopus artists splash their ink,
Creating art that makes you think.

Waves Whispering Secrets

The waves giggle as they roll,
Whipping past in playful stroll.
They tell secrets full of glee,
Of fish who dance under the sea.

Seagulls laugh with squawks so loud,
Joining in with a cheeky crowd.
The surf tickles sandy toes,
As crabs compose their silly prose.

Currents of Distant Horizons

On a surfboard, I might glide,
With dolphins joining in my ride.
We race the wind, we chase the sun,
Splashing joy, oh what a fun!

The horizon twists like a twirling cat,
Calling all to join the spat.
Pelicans diving with silly flair,
Making waves without a care.

The Heartbeats of Marine Mysteries

In the depths where bubbles play,
Fish don hats, in a quirky way.
They samba dance at sunken wrecks,
Finding lost socks, oh what the heck!

Jellyfish float with graceful flair,
While seaweed slaps like crazy hair.
Crabs pinch jokes with a cheery grin,
And starfish sing about their kin.

Unseen Paths Beneath the Waves

Beneath the ripples, secrets lie,
Octopuses sneak with a winked eye.
They dig for treasure, then play charades,
Movements so funny, like silly parades.

Barnacles gossip on the old logs,
While pufferfish juggle with bemused frogs.
In this murky world of playful sights,
Dance the nights away, under moonlit lights.

Calligraphy of the Ocean Floor

Each grain of sand tells a joke so sly,
Seahorses hover, and dolphins fly.
Seashells giggle; they wiggle and spin,
Crafting bold stories from deep within.

Starfish doodle on rock's soft face,
Drifting in slow-motion, a comical race.
Pickled sea cucumbers roll in delight,
Finding old treasures while staying out of sight.

Mariner's Lament

Oh, the sailor forgot his lunch,
A sandwich washed away with a punch.
Seagulls laugh as they snatch it right,
While fish below do the belly flop fight.

Waves crash in with a raucous cheer,
As sailors mutter with half a beer.
Pirates dance with a skip and a twirl,
But all they find is a salty pearl.

Echoes of the Saltwater Heart

The seagulls squawk like they own the place,
Stealing crumbs with a cheeky grace.
Fish in the deep wear fancy hats,
Debating who's best – the slim or the fat.

Waves tickle the sand, pulling back with giggles,
Shells join in, making silly wiggles.
A dolphin dives, but trips on a wave,
Making a splash, oh what a brave!

Dance of the Moonlit Waters

The moon grins wide, on a silver ride,
Finding fish who are trying to hide.
Crabs do the cha-cha on the warm shore,
While starfish applaud, wanting more!

A whale sings low, a curious tune,
Bubbles dancing beneath the moon.
Jellyfish waltz with glimmers and glee,
While clams pinch toes, oh, let them be!

The Infinite Blue Embrace

In the deep blue, a treasure chest waits,
Filled with rubber ducks and silly plates.
An octopus juggles, oh what a sight,
Its eight arms flailing, with all of its might.

Crabs wear sunglasses, lounging with flair,
While shrimp throw a party without a care.
The seaweed dances, a green little star,
Enticing the fish to laugh from afar!

Lullabies of the Rolling Deep

The waves hum softly, a sleepy old tune,
While fishy friends dream beneath the moon.
A sleepy seal snores with a belly so round,
While jellybeans drift, round and round.

The starfish nod, while barnacles snore,
As the ocean whispers, 'You'll soon want more.'
A crab tells a tale with a flick of its claw,
Leaving everyone laughing, in awe of its flaw!

The Mirage of the Distant Horizon

A seagull stole my sandwich, oh dear,
It laughed as it flew, oh what a sheer.
The waves danced and shimmered, quite surreal,
Was that a boat or just my meal's appeal?

Far off the sky looked like a giant plate,
I squinted hard, but couldn't quite relate.
Maybe it's lunch that I've yet to find,
Or just a mirage playing tricks on my mind.

Calm After the Roar

The storm was wild, it took my hat,
Now it's swimming with the fish and that's a spat.
But here I stand with sandy toes,
Feeling fancy as the breeze softly blows.

The sun peeks out with a wink and a grin,
I chase a crab, oh where to begin?
With laughter ringing through the salty air,
I might just start a crabby affair!

Conversations with the Driftwood

I sat with driftwood, it had much to say,
About its travels from far away.
It told me tales of ships and storms,
Of pirates and seaweed—in quirky forms!

The barnacles chimed in, making it a crowd,
Each with a story, funny and loud.
They argued about who was the best of them all,
While I just chuckled at my driftwood ball.

Reflections on the Ever-Changing Tide

I pondered life as the waves rolled in,
Wondering if crabs can ever wear a pin.
Oh, how I wish they'd dress up just right,
In tiny suits for a seafood night!

The water plays games, keeps me on my toes,
With each splash a new adventure grows.
As I laugh at the tales that the sea uncovers,
I'm convinced that the ocean's just full of lovers.

The Canvas of Neptune's Dreams

Under the waves, the fish paint a scene,
With brushes of seaweed, and colors so keen.
A crab in a beret, feeling so grand,
Creates masterpieces with a flick of his hand.

The octopus wears spectacles, reading the foam,
While starfish debate who will take the throne.
Gull's cackle echoes, a laugh so profound,
As dolphins breakdance, on the sandy ground.

Mists of the Morning Tide

The seagulls are gossiping all through the mist,
Comparing their feathers; it's quite a twist.
A clam dropped a secret just out of reach,
Now everyone's curious, but no one will breach.

Starfish arranging a game of charades,
While shrimp, like conspirators, huddle in shades.
Laughter erupts as a whale cracks a joke,
Who knew the deep blue could make such a poke?

Resonance of Deep Blue Dreams

The jellyfish jive in a rhythm so neat,
While sea urchins dance on their tiny, sharp feet.
A turtle in shades says, 'Let's ride a wave!'
But ends up doing flips, oh the laughter it gave!

Angelfish gossip in glittery schools,
While clowns decked in stripes play the funniest fools.
They juggle with pearls, make a splash here and there,
In this underwater circus, laughter fills the air.

Currents of Change and Wonder

A shrimp with a trumpet announces the news,
That crabs will be hosting a waltz with a snooze.
But fish in tuxedos glide to the beat,
Swapping their costumes — oh, what a treat!

The sea cucumbers are quite underdressed,
As tides keep on swirling, they wriggle, distressed.
But a whale with a top hat proclaims it's alright,
And everyone dances till the end of the night!

A Symphony of Distant Shores

A seagull took my sandwich, oh dear,
He laughed as he flew, a snack pioneer!
Fishes gossip in bubbles, what a sight,
While crabs do the cha-cha beneath the moonlight.

The shells hold secrets, they whisper and chime,
"Did you hear the one about the fish and the lime?"
Wave after wave, they tumble and tease,
While starfish throw parties and dance with the breeze.

The Endless Dance of Foam and Sky

The foam does a jig on the pebbly sands,
While jellyfish waltz with invisible hands.
A barnacle's boogie, a surfboard's delight,
As waves wiggle by, a hilarious sight.

Clouds wear their sunglasses, lounging all day,
While the sun flips a pancake in glittering play.
The ocean hums tunes, a bubbly refrain,
As crabs juggle shells in a comical vein.

Ebb and Flow of Forgotten Dreams

A starfish once dreamed of being a king,
With a crown made of bubbles, oh what a bling!
The waves giggled softly, tickling his pride,
As seaweed danced round him, his loyal bride.

Old driftwood tells tales of days long ago,
When fish wore top hats and mermaids would glow.
The sea laughs out loud, a humorous tone,
At dreams washed ashore, making it their own.

Beneath the Stars, the Water Stirs

Beneath twinkling stars, a crab tells a joke,
While dolphins roll laughter in waves, smoke and folk.
The moon grins a smile, like a big silver pie,
As otters build castles, oh look, they get high!

The tide tickles toes, a silly delight,
While clams sing their songs, under cover of night.
An octopus juggles glowing sea pearls,
In a world full of joy, where laughter unfurls.

Secrets Beneath the Surface

Bubbles rise in a fishy dance,
As crabs wear hats, they take a chance.
The starfish plays guitar with glee,
But jellyfish just float, carefree.

An octopus flirts with a bright red shoe,
Says, 'It's my color, looks good, don't you?'
With slippery slides, they glide with cheer,
And shout, 'Come join, we've got cold beer!'

The Ocean's Timeless Breath

Waves roll in with a silly laugh,
The dolphins play at their own behalf.
With surfboards made of seaweed and stone,
They've crafted a vibe to call their own.

Seagulls squawk, 'Where's my sandwich, dude?'
While fish in bow ties are feeling rude.
The mermaids chuckle, making a scene,
And fish in tuxedos just sip their green.

Storms That Shape the Coastline

The clouds gather for a game of bluff,
While the sea whispers, 'I've had enough!'
Raindrops dance like a tap on glass,
As waves rise up, a comedic mass.

The sandcastles wobble with a grin,
As kids run off—let the games begin!
It's nature's party, loud and wild,
With laughing whales as the honored child.

Serenity in the Depths

Beneath the waves, a quiet jester,
A clownfish dons a festive tester.
With bubbles plump and fins on show,
He jigs and wiggles in the flow.

Anemones sway, caught in giggles,
While shrimps do salsa, doing wiggles.
Oh, the ocean's calm, a joyful jest,
Where even the seaweed dances best!

Salt and Serenity

A seagull swoops, takes my fries,
I laugh as it squawks, no surprise.
Crabs dance sideways, quite the sight,
In this salty realm, everything's light.

Shells whisper secrets, not too profound,
Each grain of sand is where laughs abound.
I trip on a wave, land with a splash,
Nature's joke, always making me dash.

The Call of the Abyssal Dream

A rubber duck floats past the shore,
As fish all giggle, wanting more.
The octopus spins in a grand ballet,
While I just watch, amused, all day.

Mermaids wink, flip their long hair,
With dolphins buzzing like they don't care.
Zebra-striped seaweed does a twist,
In this underwater world, smiles persist.

In Pursuit of the Shifting Sands

Footprints disappear with each wave's charm,
Like they're playing hide-and-seek, alarm!
Kites fly high, caught in the breeze,
While I chase seagulls that always tease.

The sandcastle's a fortress, yet it's quite small,
With a brave flag that seems to stall.
I take a sip, it's salty, oh dear,
Turns out I mistook my drink for the pier!

Shimmering Reflections of the Moonlit Waves

Moonbeams dance on the laughing tide,
While crabs clap joyfully, side by side.
Jellyfish waltz in a jelly-like way,
It's a shimmering show, all here to stay.

The stars above wink, don't be shy,
As boats bob gently, like dreams in the sky.
I toast to the night with a soda can,
To the humor of the sea, oh what a plan!

The Kaleidoscope of the Ocean's Heart

In the depths where fish wear hats,
Jellybeans swim with chitchat.
Octopuses dance in polka dots,
Seahorse races in bowler knots.

Crabs in suits with little ties,
Snail mail sent from clams nearby.
A starfish flips a pancake flop,
While whales do the conga and hop.

Every wave a giggle or two,
As mermaids sing in shades of blue.
Barnacles tap to a quirky beat,
Salty laughter roams the street.

In this world where silliness flows,
The ocean's heart just loves to pose.
With winks and nods, it pulls us near,
A wavy fun that brings good cheer.

Whirls and Whispers of the Great Beyond

A dolphin jumps with goofy grace,
A narwhal's smile, a silly face.
Barnacles sport a cape in style,
The underwater mirth, a mile!

Whale fins wave like they just don't care,
A sea sponge's giggle fills the air.
Anglerfish tell jokes in the dark,
While turtles nod, it's quite the lark!

Glowing jellyfish in a dance-off,
Doing the limbo, oh, to scoff!
Mermaids chuckling, their hair in twirls,
As crabs strut by in a sassy swirl.

In currents where fun never ends,
The ocean's party, where joy transcends.
With every splash, there's laughter free,
As fish don outfits, just wait and see!

Symphony of the Unfathomable

In a sea where silly notes are found,
A fish conducts a magical sound.
With bubbles popping like confetti,
Clams join in with voices steady.

Guitars made from seaweed green,
Harmonicas that's made from a bean.
The crabs on maracas, what a tune!
As dolphins spin in a salty boon.

Every wave plays a funny beat,
With stingrays tapping their little feet.
A pitcher plant sings with delight,
While pufferfish give a giggly fright!

Their laughter echoes through the foam,
An underwater concert, a home.
The symphony of ups and downs,
Bringing giggles all around the towns.

Mists Over the Cerulean Abyss

Foggy whispers hide and seek,
Surprising fish with every peek.
A manta ray plays hideaway,
While gobies pout, 'It's not our day!'

The quaint squid with polka dots,
Revealed to us by savvy thoughts.
Turtles giggle in the misty gloom,
As orcas glide to a boisterous tune.

In this land where secrets sway,
Finding treasure is quite the play.
With each shell found, a royal laugh,
As fish parade, a goofy staff.

The ocean's veil, a laugh so sly,
Tickles the waves that wave goodbye.
Jokes slip through the moonlit glow,
In this realm, the fun will flow.

The Veil Between the Waters

Behold the fish, they wear a hat,
They swim and giggle, just like a cat.
A jellyfish serves cucumber bites,
While crabs toss jokes on moonlit nights.

The shrimp tap dance on the sandy floor,
While sea cucumbers explore the shore.
A clam tells tales of the ocean's jest,
In waters where laughter is always pressed.

A turtle spins tales, slow yet bright,
Of gulls that swoop with comical might.
A seal juggles shells, what a sight to see,
As laughter rolls in with the salty spree.

Bubbles rise high, in giggling streams,
Coral reefs echo the ocean's dreams.
So dive right in, join the fun parade,
In waters where silliness is hand-made.

Canvas of the Endless Horizon

The sky paints colors with a wink,
As dolphins skate, they pause and think.
They plan a canvas with splashes bright,
For fish who dream under the moonlight.

Sea stars come out in a sketchy line,
Each one a sketch of a quirky design.
They giggle and twirl, dance in the spray,
As the ocean brushes the clouds away.

The striped fish sport a funky style,
In polka dots, they swim a mile.
Hiding behind waves, they play a prank,
Cause bubbles to pop, in a ticklish rank.

A sand crab builds castles high and proud,
With a pompous shell, oh he's so loud!
Yet when the wave comes, he runs like a child,
In a flurry of sand, so carefree and wild.

Songs of the Sirens in Dusk's Glow

Oh the sirens sing in a playful key,
With gurgling laughter, they splash with glee.
They toss seashells like a song on air,
With notes that ripple, dance without a care.

They lure the boats with a jazzy tune,
While octopuses join in, won't be immune.
With a wave of their tentacles, they play along,
Creating melodies that feel so strong.

The crabs tap their claws, keep the beat,
As fishes float like flutes in the heat.
Undersea parties, a quirky affair,
With mermaids spinning, what a vibrant flair.

But be warned, dear sailor, watch your course,
For laughter can lead you, like a powerful force.
As jesters of water, they weave their charm,
In playful currents, it's hard to stay calm.

Reflections of a Wandering Heart

A lone seagull dances with a flair,
It twirls with a fish, a duo so rare.
They plot to sail on a floating log,
While snickering at a passing frog.

With shells for seats and seaweed ties,
They ride the waves, under sunny skies.
But oh, the antics, the giggles abound,
As they chase jellybeans that swim around.

A porpoise leaps with a cheeky grin,
Splashing the gull, oh, where to begin?
With eyes aglow, they draft a dream,
To build a boat from a melted ice cream.

Join in the fun, let the heart roam free,
In a world of laughter, come swim with me.
For reflections shimmer in the ocean's heart,
Where every wave whispers a playful start.

Whispers of the Ocean's Embrace

The fish wear hats and dance all night,
They twirl and spin in the soft moonlight.
A crab on drums plays a silly beat,
While dolphins giggle, oh what a treat!

The octopus sings, a croaky tune,
With seaweed hair, looking like a cartoon.
Jellyfish float, so graceful and free,
Tickling the toes of a curious sea.

A clam jokes loud, but no one can hear,
Seagulls snicker, they're here for a cheer.
A treasure chest full of jellybeans,
The best kind of loot for ocean scenes!

With bubbles and laughter, the sea is a show,
Where laughter and whimsy unfailingly flow.
Join in the fun, forget all the stress,
For in ocean's arms, it's all just a mess!

Currents of the Infinite Deep

The kraken's tea party is quite the affair,
With scones and jam, and seaweed in hair.
A shark wears a tie, all dapper and neat,
Inviting the turtles to join for a treat.

Whales tell the jokes, their voices so deep,
While starfish giggle, 'just don't fall asleep!'
The bubbles they blow are shapes and designs,
Like essay doodles on old water vines.

The sea cucumber offers a dance,
In wiggly moves that could put you in trance.
While pufferfish puff, trying to impress,
With their spiky charm, they're a real mess!

A clam chorus sings, off-key, loud,
As fish in bow ties perform for the crowd.
In this splashy show of giggles and glee,
Life underneath is as wild as can be!

Waves of Eternal Whisper

Under the waves, it's a wild disco,
Where eels shimmy and crabs steal the show.
The flounders flip, with feet oh so funny,
While sea cucumbers dream of making money!

Starfish play cards, but they never can win,
They joke, 'We have five, but we can't play in.'
With shells full of laughter, they gather around,
To spin tales of treasure that never are found.

A whale in a tux prances by with a flare,
Singing of soggy popcorn that makes you beware.
A dolphin breaks in, with a flip of the tail,
Proclaiming that jelly is the new holy grail!

In waters so silly, where pranks are the norm,
Even the currents seem to twist and transform.
Let's all make a splash, spread the joy like confetti,
As we drift in mirth, our hearts feel so ready!

Dance of the Celestial Waters

In a ballroom of bubbles, the fish waltz around,
While octopuses munch on the snacks that they've found.

A crab with a cane takes the lead in the dance,
While turtles groove slow in a sweet, subtle prance.

The sea urchins spin, but get tangled up tight,
Squeezing their bristles in sheer delight.
A blast from a clam sets the rhythm in motion,
As they twirl in delight, causing a commotion.

The plankton twinkles, like stars in the night,
While fish throw confetti, oh what a sight!
With laughter that echoes from reef to the shore,
This dance of the waters leaves us wanting more!

So come join the fun, let your worries all cease,
As we sway with the currents, and move with the breeze.
In the depths of the ocean, where silliness flows,
The dance of the sea is where joy always grows!

Elysium Found in the Surf

In the tide, a crab did dance,
He wore a shell, thought it romance.
But as he pranced and spun around,
He tripped on seaweed, lost his crown.

A seagull swooped, with quite a squawk,
Stealing fries from a nearby dock.
The fish all giggled, rolled their eyes,
As splashes echoed hearty sighs.

Bubbles popped with silly glee,
As kids made castles, proud at sea.
A mermaid winked, gave them a cheer,
But forgot her shell, oh dear, oh dear!

So here we splash, and here we play,
Living in joy, come what may.
With laughter loud, we ride the foam,
In our fun-filled ocean home.

Moonbeams on Silken Foam

The moonlight glints on waves like dream,
A fishy fellow starts to beam.
He tells a tale of love and fate,
While wearing shades, looking quite great.

The crabs conspire to sing a tune,
While searching for lost jellybeans in June.
They rock the sand with flair and style,
As mermaids clap, enjoying the mile.

A dolphin jumps, thinks he's a star,
He prances high, but lands too far.
The crowd just laughs, with joy in hearts,
Ocean's stage, a million arts.

With brilliance bright, the night unfolds,
As silly secrets the sea holds.
We laugh, we dance, under the dome,
In the glimmer, we find our home.

Secrets Carried by the Ripples

Whispers float on bubbly streams,
The ocean shares her silliest dreams.
A fish with glasses takes a look,
Wonders where the bookworm took a hook.

A starfish sketches on the sand,
Creating art that's slightly bland.
With every wave, it shifts and swirls,
The sea just laughs, while time unfurls.

A boat with llamas sails afar,
Each one a captain, what bizarre!
They toast with seaweed, munch on foam,
In crazy tales together they roam.

As droplets wink and giggles rise,
Life's little wonders fill our skies.
The sea is rife with jokes and fun,
A playground bright, for everyone.

Unwritten Tales of Nautical Night

With stars aglow, the sea does grin,
Unlocking giggles held within.
Octopus wearing a bright bowtie,
Tells knock-knock jokes that make us cry.

A ship made of marshmallows drifts,
Giving out candy, the best of gifts.
Pirates with hiccups sing off-key,
While jellyfish dance just for free.

The tides bring tidbits, oh what a sight,
As sea cucumbers join in the fight.
Against the crabs with silly hats,
In the great ocean, it's all about spats!

So gather 'round, let stories flow,
Of fishy friends and laughs aglow.
As waves take flight, and joy ignites,
Unwritten tales in endless nights.

Prism of the Ocean's Gaze

A crab in a tux, what a sight to see,
Dancing in shells, full of glee.
Fish in bow ties, they swim with flair,
Hosting a party, with seabed fare.

Jellyfish float, like balloons so bright,
Wiggling their tentacles, oh, what a night!
Starfish twirl, with serene delight,
While seagulls strut, and join the fight.

Each wave brings laughter, a splashy jest,
With octopuses plotting funny quests.
Seashells giggle, as the bubbles rise,
In the watery world of silly ties.

So, take a dive, come join the jest,
Under the sea, where fun is the best!
With laughter afloat, let worries cease,
In the ocean's dance, find your peace!

The Solstice of Waves and Dreams

Here comes a seal, with a surfboard wide,
Sliding on waves, with a quirky glide.
Seagulls in shades give him a cheer,
While dolphins jump, with a splash and sneer.

Mermaids gossip, their tails entwined,
Plotting a game, the best you'll find.
With clams as maracas, they sing out loud,
A concert of laughter, drawing a crowd.

A starfish shrugs, in a funny pose,
As barnacles giggle, in their crusty rows.
The seaweed sways to the giggly beat,
While crabs bring chips, a crunchy treat!

So let the waves bring joy anew,
With dreams that sparkle in ocean's blue.
In this playful realm, no gloom shall be,
Join in the fun, dance wild and free!

Woven Stories of the Abyss

A wise old turtle, in shades of jade,
Tales of the ocean, effortlessly made.
With hiccups of laughter, he shares his lore,
About a fish that wore a hat and nothing more.

Octopuses giggle, playing hide and seek,
Amongst the corals, so bright and sleek.
A shrimp with a trumpet, gives a bold show,
While sea cucumbers just lie there, so slow.

The flounders flip, in a clumsy ballet,
Creating a splash, like a watery play.
The anglerfish winks, with a glimmering hook,
Inviting the night, for a thrilling look.

Bubbles float up, carrying seeds of fun,
In tales of the deep, where dreams are spun.
With humor and joy, the ocean's a fest,
Where every wave invites you for a jest!

The Lore of the Wind and Water

Oh, the wind whispers secrets, to the sea so blue,
Of a pirate's lost socks, and a whale that flew.
With waves crashing laughter on a sandy shore,
Every breeze brings giggles, who could ask for more?

Seagulls squawk jokes, from their lofty stage,
About crabs in a race, who turned the wrong page.
The winds twist and twirl, in a hilarious chase,
While all of the fishes just roll in their space.

A pelican lands, with a splash and a thud,
Carrying stories, both silly and crud.
As the moonlight dances, the ocean grins wide,
In this funny realm, there's nothing to hide.

So, join in the laughter, and let worries flee,
In the whimsical waves, find your glee.
With each gust of wind, let joy take flight,
In the stories of water, all is just right!

Tempests and Tranquilities

The waves roll in with a giggling spree,
Crashing on rocks like a slapstick spree.
Seagulls squawk as they take to the air,
While fish flip-flop like they just don't care.

Buckets and spades clog the sandy line,
Children shriek as they jump to the brine.
A crab waves claws in a silly ballet,
As sunburned tourists get lost in the spray.

Balloons float off, oh what a dance!
While sandcastles melt in a watery trance.
Pirates debate if they'll steal a quick snack,
But the treasure's just chips in a crinkly pack.

Yet through the chaos, a calmness prevails,
As laughter sails high on the breezy gales.
For even the storms can bring a good cheer,
With friendly foolery docked ever near.

Songs of the Open Waters

Drifting along, a rubber duck sings,
To a chorus of gulls on their wobbly wings.
A dolphin splashes with flamboyant flair,
While a seashell debates if it's really all there.

Mermaids gossip with seaweed in tow,
Trading mascara tips for a wave and a blow.
A swaggering crab with a gem on its claw,
Turns into a star; who'd have thought it could draw?

Nautical nonsense swirls in the breeze,
As jellyfish jiggle like soft, slippery cheese.
Yakety-yak from an octopus band,
Plays jazzy tunes made of ocean and sand.

With gales of laughter spilling so free,
It's a riotous opera beneath our grand sea.
Through mishaps and splashes, we twirl and we sway,
In this silly concert, we dance through the gray.

Cascades of Celestial Light

Stars flicker down like dramatic cues,
While moonbeams dance in their whimsical shoes.
A mermaid swirls through the shimmering glow,
With a wink and a giggle as she steals the show.

The night is alive with chuckles and charm,
As sea creatures plot to create a huge farm.
Flounders proclaim they're the stars of the night,
In costumes absurd, it's a comical sight.

Bonkers sea turtles toss jellybean treats,
While clownfish swim with their bright, silly feats.
Starfish put on a talent show spree,
And octopuses juggle with joy oh so free.

As laughter cascades from the depths of the sea,
With thrill-seeking dolphins, we're wild and carefree.
A twinkling spectacle none could foresee,
Lost in the glow of a funny jubilee.

The Transience of Shoreline Dreams

Footprints trace stories that wash far away,
Like a whimsical tale of the dogs gone astray.
Seagulls are searching for fries on the beach,
While a clam tries to imitate stars in their speech.

Sandcastles tend to sway with the breeze,
As kids feed their shovels with giggles and sneezes.
A kite takes flight, doing loop-de-loop spins,
While the tide rolls in with waves full of grins.

In the chaos of charms, mermaids blend in,
Cackling with seals who just cannot win.
With a swaggering fish in a top hat so dapper,
Proclaiming, "I'm here for the seaweed and caper!"

But as the sun sets and the shadows elongate,
The ocean takes back all its playful fate.
With dreams washed away, like flights of the breeze,
We'll return to the shore with our memories, at ease.

The Echo of Distant Cries

Upon the shore, a seagull squawks,
Breezes steal my sandwich, what a hoax!
With salty hair and sand-filled shoes,
I chase the waves while sipping brew.

The crabs are plotting, I swear it's true,
In a line dance, they're making their debut.
The ocean laughs with each splash and foam,
I'm just a beach bum, far from home.

A fish swims by with a goofy grin,
Waving hello with a fin, oh what a spin!
I toss a pebble, it ricochets wide,
Only to land in a seagull's ride.

As sunset paints the sky with flair,
The jellyfish are doing their hair.
With bubbles popping like party balloons,
I hum a tune to the ocean's tunes.

Breaths of the Untamed Ocean

The waves come in with a silly rush,
Squid play tag in a bubbling hush.
I dived on in, with squeaky glee,
Only to find a fish that won't flee.

My floaty's lost to a cautious whale,
It giggles hard, I start to flail.
With each big splash, I'm sure to declare,
I'm the captain of this rubbery chair!

The snorkeling gear is a sight to behold,
With my mask on, I feel so bold.
But as I trip over a starfish star,
The sea is laughing, echoing afar.

As jellybeans float in the ocean wide,
I fear I may have swallowed some tide.
But on this adventure, I'll take the fall,
With a chuckle, the sea sings to all.

Sailing the Dream-Stirred Waters

On a raft made of old pizza boxes,
I sail the waves while dodging hawks' flocks.
A banana as my trusty mast,
With a crew of crabs, we're having a blast.

My compass spun like a dizzy song,
It pointed everywhere, oh so wrong!
A dolphin flips with a wink and grin,
"Join my crew!" it said with a spin.

With snacks on deck and no fish in sight,
We chart our course by moon's soft light.
But a wave tickled and stole my hat,
The seagulls shrieked, "You call that a spat?"

O, treasure maps of candy and cheer,
I think we're lost, but let's have a beer!
In dream-stirred waters, we laugh in delight,
This voyage may just end up quite right.

Fragments of Time Beneath the Waves

Beneath the waves, a watch does tick,
But it's a fish's, and it's just for kicks.
With fins that flip and bubbles that toss,
They gossip of marbles, of who's the boss.

A seaweed wig holds court like a king,
While clams are debating the latest bling.
An octopus shares tales of lost socks,
"Beware the shore where they stash in blocks!"

A turtle munches on ancient lore,
A snack of seafoam and tales galore.
With each ripple of laughter and quirks,
The clocks can't keep up with underwater perks.

So let's dive deep, where the laughter swells,
Amongst funny fish and their shimmery spells.
In fragments of moments, let's celebrate,
For each silly splash, oh, isn't this great?

Tales of the Rising Moon

There once was a crab, with a hat,
Who dreamt he could dance like a cat.
He twirled on the sand,
With a drink in his hand,
But ended up flat on his back.

A seagull, so wise, shared a wink,
While stealing the fish from my sink.
"Don't bother with nets,
Just offer them Bets!"
And soon I was left with a pink drink.

The dolphins held parties at night,
With confetti of shells, what a sight!
They sang silly songs,
And danced all night long,
Till morning brought in the first light.

So if you should sneak by the coast,
Beware of the crab who may boast.
He'll invite you to strut,
In a shell-boat so cut,
And laugh till you both need a toast!

The Color of Dusk on the Water

At sunset the fish wear a grin,
In pajamas made out of thin skin.
They giggle and splash,
In a wild, fishy clash,
While the octopus twirls with a spin.

A starfish once claimed he could sing,
But all that he did was flapping,
Still, every shell cheered,
As the seaweed neared,
Bringing snacks, which he found quite captivating.

The sun slipped away like a slide,
As crabs toasted marshmallows with pride.
They roasted them light,
By the glow of the night,
Claiming sea salt was all they applied.

With laughter that echoed afar,
They played games, and danced by a star.
When the moon took its throne,
They felt quite at home,
With jokes by the tide and a jar!

Journey of Solitude in the Surf

I ventured alone with my kite,
But the wind had a different delight.
It lifted me high,
Into the bright sky,
While seagulls below looked in fright.

The waves whispered tales of the past,
But my flip-flops flew off way too fast.
They joined with a fish,
Who made a big wish,
For a day that wouldn't be outclassed.

As I chased all my shoes through the foam,
I thought that I'd surely go home.
But a dolphin said, "Nay!
Let's dance and play!"
Then laughed as he made me his comb.

So I laughed as the sea called my name,
In this wild, wacky game I became.
With flips and with spins,
No losses, just wins,
My solo to surf was aflame!

Whispers of a Forgotten Shore

On a shore where the sands like to chat,
I met a wise old crab named Pat.
He said with a cheer,
"Come on over here,
And help me to dance on my mat!"

The shells held a raucous debate,
About which one of them was first rate.
With each little click,
They grew brave and quick,
Till the beach turned into a state.

A jellyfish spun tales of the sun,
In a costume so bright, oh what fun!
He glided with grace,
In a whimsical race,
Till the tide told him, "You're done!"

So we gathered our laughter and joy,
With each wave that bounced like a toy.
As the moon came to play,
In a grand ballet,
We danced, oh what bliss to enjoy!

Uncharted Currents of the Soul

There once was a fish with a hat,
He thought he could dance, but he sat.
Around him, they swam,
Chasing dreams like a spam.

Uncharted Currents of the Soul

A crab wrote a map made of cheese,
He dreamed of the land of the bees.
The bees, they disagreed,
And left him to plead.

Uncharted Currents of the Soul

Dolphins played cards near a reef,
They dealt out their hands, full of grief.
But the octopus won,
With eight arms for fun.

Uncharted Currents of the Soul

Seagulls were squawking a tune,
They danced 'round the sun like a balloon.
But one took a dive,
And missed the high-five.

Celestial Ripples on the Canvas of Time

The stars in the sky became bold,
They twinkled and laughed, legends told.
But a comet flew by,
And made everyone cry.

Celestial Ripples on the Canvas of Time

An astronaut tripped on a star,
He stumbled, and that was bizarre.
He floated with flair,
And lost his space chair.

Celestial Ripples on the Canvas of Time

Planets were playing a game,
Each one was trying for fame.
But black holes would cheat,
And eat all the heat.

Celestial Ripples on the Canvas of Time

The sun wore a pair of bright shades,
While warming the world on parades.
The clouds rolled their eyes,
As thunder disguised.

The Horizon's Silent Song

A turtle tried singing aloud,
But no one could tell, it was proud.
With a melody strange,
He swam through the change.

The Horizon's Silent Song

A whale formed a band with a fish,
They played every note, what a swish.
But the gulls stole the show,
And danced to and fro.

The Horizon's Silent Song

A seaweed conductor gets loud,
While jellyfish sway with the crowd.
They cheer as they sway,
In their own little way.

The Horizon's Silent Song

Starfish became hip-hop stars,
Rapping in time, they ate jars.
With each funky beat,
They made waves in the heat.

Beneath the Surface

Bubbles formed thoughts of delight,
A pufferfish giggled all night.
With each jabbering burst,
He dodged every thirst.

Beneath the Surface

An eel wore a flashy pink tie,
As he wriggled and rolled, oh so spry.
The fish shouted, 'Hey!'
'Who invited this gay?'

Beneath the Surface

A clam tried his best to be hip,
He invited a starfish for a trip.
But when it was time,
He forgot the rhyme.

Beneath the Surface

An octopus juggled some pearls,
While tickling all of the girls.
With eight arms so deft,
It laughed at the left!

Shadows Stir

In the depths where shadows do dance,
A grouper took part in romance.
With whispers so sweet,
He lost to a tweet.

Shadows Stir

A ghostly fish glimmered with fright,
He scared all the shrimp in one night.
As they swam away fast,
He chuckled at last.

Shadows Stir

A rogue wave played hide and seek,
As seahorses laughed every week.
But when found in a twist,
They flopped as they missed.

Shadows Stir

The squid threw a party, oh neat,
With snacks made of brine and old meat.
But the jellyfish fled,
As they danced with the dead.

The Call of Distant Shores

The gulls are squawking, what a show,
As beach balls bounce from toe to toe.
An octopus plays hide and seek,
While sunburnt tourists squeal and squeak.

With every wave that rolls ashore,
A crab's got more than one claw to score.
Yet laughter echoes, shadows throng,
As flip-flops dance to a silly song.

A fish in a sunhat, what a sight,
Winking at swimsuits, gleaming bright.
Sandcastles topple with a splash,
As waves applaud with a joyful crash.

Oh, the beach is quite the silly place,
With jellyfish jiving in a graceful race.
As sunshine giggles, humor swells,
In this ocean of laughter, all is well.

Ciphers in the Sand

Footprints zigzag like a madman's map,
Saying 'hello' with a sandy clap.
A dolphin giggles just out of view,
While seagulls squawk their witty brew.

Messages whispered by the waves,
In this sandy land of joyous knaves.
A starfish dons a floppy hat,
To shade its eyes from sunlit chat.

Shells gather secrets of salty lore,
As tide pools giggle at the shore.
With every wave, a tale they weave,
In this tale of sand where all believe.

So grab your spade and join the game,
In this ciphered fun without the fame.
For laughter's written, plain as day,
In the grains where sun and sea kids play.

Embraces of Changing Winds

Breezes laugh and tickle the trees,
As kites soar high with utmost ease.
The wind whispers jokes through the air,
Causing hats to dance without a care.

A beachcomber spots a wig on a wave,
Ultimately claiming it as his brave.
With sand in socks and joy in a cart,
The ocean's embrace warms the heart.

Winds blow scents of cotton candy,
Tickling noses, oh so handy.
The surf joins in, with a sly little gig,
As swimmers wade with a playful jig.

Even sea turtles look amused,
When the gulls strut in their fanciest shoes.
In this merry mix of nature's tune,
We dance with the winds from morn till moon.

Waves of Forgotten Souls

Lost flip-flops wander, seeking feet,
While beach chairs gossip and laugh with heat.
An old crab tells tales of days gone by,
With seaweed wigs and a wink of an eye.

The waves frolic, teasing the rest,
"Don't forget your sunscreen, that's the best!"
Laughing at memories caught in the spray,
Dancing shadows that drift away.

Sandy sculptures seem misaligned,
As merry ghosts join the beach, combined.
With laughter echoing from dusk till dawn,
These forgotten souls have a lively con.

Beneath the Veil of the Deep Blue

Under the waves where fishies play,
A mermaid forgot her own birthday.
She tried to bake with seaweed and sand,
But all she got was a jellyfish band.

A crab in a top hat danced on the floor,
Telling dad jokes, we all want more.
While seahorses giggle, the octopus swings,
Complaining the world isn't ready for kings.

Gulls steal their lunch, so clever and sly,
As starfish sit back, just waving goodbye.
With waves for their table, they dined by the glow,
On plankton soufflé and seaweed a la mode!

Bubbles and laughter fill ocean's halls,
As the clownfish make jokes that echo through walls.
In this deep blue realm where silliness reigns,
Underwater chuckles run wild like the trains.

Secrets of the Liquid Horizon

The ocean's a riddle that giggles and squirts,
With clams that can't keep their pearls in their shirts.
They whisper their secrets, but only to shells,
Who laugh at the gossip they heard from the swells.

The dolphins are juggling, that's quite a feat,
While penguins in tuxedos bring snacks for a treat.
Oh, what would they serve? Why, fish sticks and fries,
A feast that leaves everyone rolling in ties!

The seaweed don dresses and sways with delight,
While turtles debate who's the fastest in flight.
With jellyfish sandals that float on the breeze,
They dance round the reefs, doing flips with such ease!

Lost treasure is found—it's a rubber fish toy,
That spins and it giggles, oh what a joy!
So next time you're near, just listen and see,
The secrets that bubble beneath waves of glee.

Serenade of the Timeless Surf

In the swell of the surf, where seagulls all croon,
A clam sings a ditty beneath the bright moon.
With waves as a beat, it's a melody strange,
As fish do the tango and happily change.

The mermaids are giggling, their hair in a twist,
Making puns about land, which they can't quite resist.
A whale's in the back, with a trumpet-like blow,
Joining in chorus, stealing the show!

Crabs on the shoreline are dancing in pairs,
Wearing old sandals, with glittering wares.
As sea foam applauds, they stretch out with flair,
Performing their act for the sand dunes laid bare.

With laughter and joy, the ocean does sway,
To the serenade sung in a splashy ballet.
So if you should stroll by the shimmering surf,
Just stop and enjoy the joys of the turf.

The Enchanted Lagoon's Tale

In a lagoon where the waters do twirl,
Lived a fish with a fancy top hat and a whirl.
He thought he was charming, oh what a mistake!
As frogs croaked in laughter, they made him a cake!

With sprinkles of algae and frosting of foam,
They baked till the sun floated over their home.
As bubbles blew kisses and ripples would grin,
Each splash told a story, where fun could begin.

A turtle named Tim wore a cape made of sea,
Claiming he's faster than a deep-sea marquee.
But every time he'd race, it was never quite right,
For he tripped on a shell and gave everyone fright!

The lagoon's full of magic, where laughter is spun,
And dreams of the ocean make every day fun.
So join in the frolic, where memories sail,
In a whimsical world, you'll never find pale.

Tattoos of Salt and Foam

A seagull swoops for my sun-kissed snack,
With a squawk that echoes back.
The crabs have all made a daring retreat,
Leaving only shells for my sandy feet.

Fish parade in their scales and glee,
Whispering secrets to the briny spree.
I laugh as the waves tickle my toes,
While a jellyfish boogies and winks like it knows.

Sandcastles rise and then meet their doom,
Brought down by the ocean's frothy plume.
I draw a mermaid with a goofy grin,
While the tide rolls in and I wave, "Let's begin!"

With laughter echoing under the noon,
And flip-flops dancing to a salty tune.
Who needs a treasure when the sun will gleam,
On the salty tattoos of my ocean dream?

Underneath the Floating Stars

The moon takes a dip in the cooling brine,
While fish wear their sequins, looking divine.
Crabs host a party with shells all aglow,
Hip-hop to the rhythm of the current's flow.

A starfish sporting a hat made of shells,
Dances with seaweed, oh how it swells!
They twirl and they spin in a watery waltz,
While I giggle at sea's comical faults.

The ocean whispers tales of bizarre delight,
As sea turtles skate under the starlit night.
A porpoise joins in with tricks and some flair,
Making the waves seem debonair.

Underneath the stars that float with such grace,
Life's a big splash in this underwater race.
So tell me, dear friend, with the sea as our seat,
Who needs a plane when the tide's in our beat?

The Labyrinth of Coral Stories

Corals twist and turn, with colors so bright,
Whispering secrets in the shimmering light.
Clownfish giggle as they peek from their homes,
While sea anemones sway like flowery domes.

Octopuses juggling their shells with a grin,
As I navigate stories tucked deep within.
Each nook tells a tale, both funny and grand,
In this underwater world where cheer will expand.

A grouper tells tales of a pearl-thieved night,
While the shrimp do their cha-cha, all feeling just right.
An eel tells a joke that makes sea urchins laugh,
As I lose my way on this coral path.

With laughter and bubbles, we sip on the fun,
In the labyrinth where stories have spun.
Dive deeper and deeper, follow the glow,
For tales of the reef continue to flow.

Ebbing Memories and Flowing Thoughts

The tide ebbs back, a grumpy old friend,
Steals my sandcastle, won't make amends.
"Hey!" I shout, as it slinks out of sight,
A cheeky retreat under the moon's light.

Memories wash in with the foamy spree,
Of beach frisbees flying and giggles of glee.
Collecting the laughter from the salty air,
As seahorses bop to the tunes without care.

I found a bottle with a message inside,
It read, "Don't forget the good times," and smiled wide.
A postcard from dolphins, swimming in loops,
Saying, "Join us for coffee and seaweed scoops!"

As the oceans ebb and thoughts come to play,
I chuckle at memories that drift far away.
For in each rising wave and playful swirl,
Lies the joy of the sea in a spinning whirl.

Reflections on a Liquid Canvas

Waves giggle as they crash and foam,
A fish flips by, claiming it's home.
Seagulls squawk, on their quest for lunch,
Snatching chips, they dive in a punch!

Sandcastles rise, a glory grand,
Till a wave sneezes, and it can't stand.
"What was that?" the kids shout in glee,
"Just nature's way of throwing a spree!"

With buckets in hand, they splash and play,
The ocean laughs, mischievous all day.
"Look, a crab!" one kid gives a yell,
"I think it's hiding, oh what a shell!"

As sun dips low, the fish conspire,
To dance and twirl, to spark desire.
Tonight we feast, on laughter and cheer,
The sea's our stage, let's give a cheer!

Celestial Ripples

Stars dance above in a shimmering trance,
While moonbeams challenge waves to prance.
"A splash contest!" the ocean calls,
As crabs wear crowns and the seaweed sprawls.

From beach to the sky, the laughter's clear,
Jellyfish jiggle, tickled with cheer.
"Catch me if you can!" they seem to say,
As they float on by in a wobbly way.

The sun starts to set, painting skies bright,
While dolphins play tag in the fading light.
"Last one in is a rotten egg!"
One shouts with glee, then takes a leg.

As the waves roll in, they burst with glee,
Bubbles and giggles fill the salty spree.
"Let's do it again!" the night air sings,
Join the parade, where laughter springs!

The Siren's Call in the Night

Under the stars, the ocean hums,
A mermaid sings, while the sea lion drums.
"Come join the dance!" she calls so sweet,
But her tail winks—oh, what a cheat!

The sailors laugh, with rum in their cups,
"For dancing with sirens, we'll never give up!"
They float and they sway, on the waves they glide,
While the mermaid giggles, flowing with pride.

"Just one more drink!" a sailor yells,
"Or maybe three! This sea casts spells!"
With shells as their hats, they all take a dive,
Chasing the bubbles, feeling alive.

The moon starts to rise, a silver sheen,
The night wraps around, cozy and keen.
"Sing us a tune!" they holler in fright,
But the mermaid just winks and swims out of sight!

Chasing Shadows on the Shore

Footprints in sand, a treasure to find,
Each wave erases what you'd left behind.
"Hey, wait for me!" cries a dog on the run,
Chasing his tail, just having some fun!

The sun dips low, painting shadows tall,
"Follow me, seagulls!" they crow, they call.
With beaks wide open, ready for fries,
A culinary hunt under wide-open skies.

"Who touched the water?" questioned a shoe,
As splashes arise, and laughter ensues.
"Not me," came replies with a giggle and grin,
As the tide teased toes and drew the line in.

With sand in their hair, and joy in their hearts,
The beach is a canvas where silliness starts.
So dance on the shore, come laugh with the tide,
For the night isn't over, let's all take a ride!

Secrets Beneath the Blue Horizon

Bubbles rise with secrets told,
Fish in hats, oh, what a sight!
Crabs dance cha-cha, oh so bold,
While starfish play cards by the light.

Gull's got jokes, feathers in a twist,
Octopus juggling, what a clown!
Don't forget the seaweed's list,
Of all the fish who act like frown!

A treasure chest with socks and more,
Lost pirate's loot from days of yore.
Shake a tail, they shout with glee,
Under the waves, life's a spree!

So dive on down, don't be shy,
Sea creatures giggle, oh my, oh my!
In this world beneath the tide,
Every splash is a joyful ride!

Echoes of the Wandering Waters

Whispers echo through the spray,
Mermaids giggle in a play.
Dolphins leap, then take a bow,
Seaweed wigs on fish, oh wow!

Waves ripple like a laughing child,
Seashells sing, the ocean wild.
Starfish gossip, crabs on phones,
Jellyfish boast of squishy thrones!

The stingrays skate in graceful loops,
Sharing tales of silly troops.
Sardines form a conga line,
Who needs a dance floor? We're just fine!

As the sun sets, colors blend,
Whimsical wonders never end.
So come, my friend, and take a dip,
Join the laughter, don't you slip!

The Horizon's Lullaby

A gentle wave hums a soft tune,
While sea cucumbers dance 'neath the moon.
Clownfish giggle, playing peek-a-boo,
Making a splash, oh what a view!

Oysters whisper secrets of old,
As krill come together, brave and bold.
Barnacles gossip on their stone,
Making the tides feel like home!

The horizon glimmers, a cheeky grin,
As seagulls race to see who can win.
A crab in a suit, all dressed up nice,
Declares a party, "Isn't this spice?"

So sway with the motion, let laughter flow,
With each ripple, the fun will grow.
A lullaby sung by the briny deep,
In this sea of joy, come take a leap!

Rhythms of the Boundless Waves

The ocean dances to its own beat,
While fish in tuxedos shuffle their feet.
With bubbles popping, joy ascends,
Under the sea, where laughter blends.

Crabs lead a conga, shells in the air,
While friendly mollusks twirl without care.
Sea horses prance, tails all entwined,
A parade of joy, what a sight to find!

The waves clap hands as they roll and swirl,
With jellyfish twirling, oh what a whirl!
Singing a song of frolic and fun,
Where salty jokes are for everyone.

So leap in the surf, let your worries fade,
In this watery world where games are played.
With each rising wave, hear the silly calls,
In the rhythm of joy, everyone sprawls!

Journey of the Wandering Waves

The waves like dancers, flapping their fin,
They waltz to the shore, then back again.
With every splash, they giggle and play,
Chasing the seagulls who think they can sway.

They flip and they flop, oh what a sight,
Crashing on rocks, then taking a flight.
But watch out beachgoers, don't let them tease,
For they'll sneak up and steal your ice cream with ease!

Rolling and laughing, they bubble with glee,
"Let's go on a picnic!" they shout from the sea.
With seaweed sandwiches, sand in each bite,
But who needs fine dining? This feels just right!

They frolic in circles, with no cares in sight,
Waves making mischief from morning 'til night.
But as the sun sets, they bid us adieu,
"Catch you tomorrow, we've got waves to brew!"

Sandcastles and Dreamscapes

In soft golden valleys where castles are grande,
A bucket and shovel, all part of the plan.
Yet each wave that rolls in brings a sneaky surprise,
"Hey, you can't catch me!" it seems to imply!

Building a fortress, watch how it gleams,
But the tide's in a hurry, or so it seems.
"Just five more minutes!" we shout to the sea,
But the waves take their cue, and laugh wild and free.

Mermaid architects in swimmies approach,
"Ooops!" one declares as she makes a slight broach.
With splashes of water and shells on the side,
The sandcastles topple, oh well, what a ride!

As sun sinks to sleep, the sea starts to yawn,
"A little more mayhem before I am gone!"
But with laughter and cheer, we build once again,
Because tomorrow, dear friends, we'll do it—amen!

Beneath the Seafoam Veil

Bubbles rise up, tickling my toes,
Where laughter and giggles beneath water flows.
Fish wave hello with spectacles on,
"Join us for tea!" they happily spawn.

The seafoam brings mischief; it tickles my chin,
"Who knew the ocean had secrets within?"
With jellyfish giggles and crabs that can dance,
There's no need for sadness; let's take a chance!

We glide with the dolphins, our joy knows no bounds,
"Let's race!" they declare, circling round.
But it's all in good fun, we're here for the show,
As they splash all around, putting on quite the glow!

A sea cucumber grins, "It's a party, you see?
Bring your laughter, it's all about glee!"
So beneath all the froth, we find blissful reprieve,
With bubbles and laughter, it's hard to believe!

Strands of Lost Memories

The shoreline is scattered with shells by the score,
Each holds a story, a tale we explore.
"Listen!" they whisper, from ages long past,
As each gentle wave makes memories last.

Old flip-flops drift softly, the lost pair of dancers,
While children make friends with imaginary pranksters.
"Remember the time when we ran from a wave?"
Those strands of nostalgia, oh how they behave!

With giggles and tales, the sand tells its truths,
While seaweed stretches like silly old youths.
"Let's name that sea turtle!" one shouts with delight,
As we sketch out our dreams in the fading daylight.

So gather your treasures, and don't let them fade,
For life is a beach, with fun surely made.
We'll spin yarns from the waves, and cherish the sea,
For memories linger, like salt from the spree!